"I CAN'T DO THIS!"

("SO...WHO WILL?")

BY ELIZABETH A. ENGKJER

"I Can't Do This!" ("So...Who Will?")

Trilogy Christian Publishers A Wholly Owned Subsidary of Trinity Broadcasting Network

2442 Michelle Drive Tustin, CA 92780

Cover design by: Kristy Swank

For information about special discounts for bulk purchases, please contact Trilogy Christian Publishing.

Trilogy Disclaimer: The views and content expressed in this book are those of the author and may not necessarily reflect the views and doctrine of Trilogy Christian Publishing or the Trinity Broadcasting Network.

Manufactured in the United States of America

10 9 8 7 6 5 4 3 2 1

Library of Congress Cataloging-in-Publication Data is available.

ISBN: 978-1-68556-913-6

E-ISBN: 978-1-68556-914-3

Elizabeth and her first English class

Dedicated to our three older grandchildren,
Landon, Cas, and Kaiya,
who came to work in Florón during the summer.
And Cindy Medema, who said long ago,
"Elizabeth, you should write a book."
And of course, to Richard, who remains my number one IT man.

TABLE OF CONTENTS

PREFACE

Taken from *The Holy Spirit and Reality* by Watchman Nee, First Edition, August 2001, published by Living Stream Ministry, Anaheim, California:

> The message in this book (i.e., "The Holy Spirit and Reality") touches a great matter in the Christian life—the Holy Spirit and reality. With concrete examples, it demonstrates that behind everything spiritual there is reality. This reality is in the Holy Spirit, and the Holy Spirit leads men into the knowledge of this reality...

I have not written or published previously. That will be apparent. The introduction and after are in my own words except for biblical quotes. I prefaced the introduction in hopes that Watchman Nee's words will more succinctly clarify my purpose, which is to unveil the incredible work of the Holy Spirit as a guide to a willing heart and to use that person to meet far-reaching goals or miracles not based on education (theological or otherwise) or intellect but solely on a fervent love for and seeking after Jesus Christ.

INTRODUCTION

Spirituality is a very personal topic and one that can remain deeply hidden within oneself and has varying meanings from individual to individual. It is not finite and thus, cannot be physically grasped or touched. And as we have become a very "hurry-scurry" society and world, spirituality may even remain tucked away within oneself. Reflecting over twenty-five years, I am sure the presence of spirituality has often been unnoticed or ignored by myself. However, over these years, there have been repeated baffling episodes and occurrences in my life that "spirituality" surfaced within, and part of that spirituality was something other than what I could attribute to myself... My hope in sharing these years will bring concrete reality with the presence of the Holy Spirit. If "spirituality" is something your hurried/pressured life has disregarded, I understand. Hanging on the wall next to our apartment door in Ecuador is a plaque that states better than I ever could,

Make time for

Quiet Moments

as *God whispers*
and the world
is loud

"Take time for Quiet Moments as God whispers and the world is loud." (No person is given credit for these words of wisdom.) My increasing "quiet moments" have uncovered within the Holy Spirit of God, who has lifted, carried, and guided me through unspeakable times of resistance, doubt, grief, and, yes, overwhelming, unspeakable joy... Our loud world seems void of experiencing and being used by the Holy Spirit of God. May you long for and take "quiet moments" and be blessed and rejuvenated to new levels in your life each day, each experience.

> *"...and He will give you another Helper, that He may*
> *abide with you forever—the Spirit of truth, whom*
> *the world cannot receive, because it neither sees Him*
> *nor knows Him; but you know Him, for He dwells*
> *with you and will be in you. I will not leave you as*
> *orphans..."*
>
> (John 14:16–18a, NKJV)

Chapter 1

"I Do Not Feel Called..."

This was the *third* time Elsie Demarest asked me to go on our church women's mission trip to Ecuador. Each time—even this third time—I tried to be polite and said I did not *feel* called to go on this mission trip (which was not medical). I am a nurse, and I had gone on two exciting medical missions in the jungle of Belize the past two summers. Even farther back, our family (my husband, I, and our three children—twelve, fourteen, and fifteen then) had gone with Christian Medical and Dental Society to Jamaica. We worked in the hurricane-ravaged, seven-floor hospital in Montego Bay. Canadians built and gifted the hospital to the people of Jamaica. I vividly recall this pathetic lady they asked me to persuade into entering the hospital and then escort up to the seventh floor... She obviously was in a deranged manic state, in a urine-soaked dress, loudly ranting, resistive, and minimally combative... I was able to coax her gently and persuasively up out of the dirt outside the hospital's ER and guide her to the seventh-floor psychiatric unit. The next day, I returned to visit her; she lay badly bruised, expressionless, and motionless on a mattress, no sheet, just a bare mattress. I was all too familiar with that distant, vacant gaze in her eyes. I knew they had "manhandled" her, unaware and untrained of how to manage someone in this state other than they had. Undoubtedly, she had been sedated with antipsychotic medication. I have worked on psychiatric units most of my nursing career...I felt "equipped," experienced, and extremely protective of people with mental health issues. People at church often come to me to share about a family member with a psych diagnosis/

disorder; individuals gravitated in my direction who had previously been hospitalized...they knew I understood and that whatever they confided would never be repeated, questioned, or criticized; I am "safe."

As I think back to when Elsie asked me to join the women's mission to Ecuador, I probably was a little too prideful, perhaps smug. I had no interest in going on this mission trip since I inwardly felt more "skilled" or "specialized" than going to paint a church, do a women's craft project, or do a Bible study. Furthermore, joining the mission did require church meetings to "prepare" for the mission trip, and it just was not my cup of tea... I am not sure why...maybe it is evident.

However, Elsie was certainly not derailed or sidetracked by my third refusal. Instead, she bristled a little and, slightly raising her voice half an octave and increasing her volume, replied, "Elizabeth, if you won't go, we have to cancel this trip because *we don't have enough people.*" At that moment, I had no idea where my response floated in from... Automatically, I replied, "Elsie, I'd love to go." This was just *not me.* To this day, I am still in disbelief at my immediate response...I am not at all a quick thinker or spontaneous with decisions; I mull things over for an exceptionally long time. Where did those words erupt from? Today...in retrospect, I am more than a little ashamed of my disinterest and dismissal of the mission... Unknowingly, Elsie's persistence began the start of a twenty-five-year project in impoverished, gang-laden, prostitute-strutting, drug-ridden, and medically-ignored squatters in the village of Florón, Ecuador.

> *"Stand at the crossroads and look; ask for the ancient*
> *paths, ask where the good way is, and walk in it..."*
> (Jeremiah 6:16, NIV)

CHAPTER 2

"I Want to Play the Guitar in Church"

That first adventuresome mission trip to Ecuador that I obviously did *not* feel called to go on introduced me to Daniel, a handsome young man with his shock of very thick, dark hair and a winsome smile that almost seemed permanently placed on his face. Daniel kept filling our paint cans as we slapped barn red paint on the church in Florón. Well into two to three hours of painting in the Ecuadorian equator sun, perspiration streaming, I noticed beyond Daniel's winsome smile.

Oh, my word, this kid doesn't have a right forearm or hand, I shockingly mused. I did not want to stare, and with a quick, inconspicuous glance, I noticed a "nub" at his elbow that he used like a very tiny finger to tip his larger paint can and replenish ours. Daniel seemed oblivious, quite confident, and comfortable with his deformity, which he did not even seem to be aware of as a "deformity." Except, at an evening church service that we attended, Daniel strode up to the front of the church and passionately declared to the congregation that he wanted Jesus to heal his arm so he could play the guitar in church. (Well, I could not wait to see how that turned out for him. Not that I do not believe in miracles today, but that was a whopper of a request!)

After no real forethought, I found myself asking the host missionaries, Pastors Rosa and Pedro del Hierro, if they thought Daniel and his parents would be in favor of him being fitted for a prosthetic arm in the USA. (Note: As I previously stated, I am an extremely cautious person. *Impulsive* does not fit me. So where did this novel idea erupt from this time?)

When I was a little girl, we lived next door to Dale and Lorraine Clark. In his teens, Dale had lost his leg from cancer and had a prosthetic leg. Now, as an adult, Dale had a thriving prosthetic clinic in Des Moines, Iowa. We always corresponded, and I was hoping they would be the perfect avenue to provide Daniel with the arm he asked for from Jesus. If Dale agreed, I would take Daniel to Iowa. However, when I later inquired, Dale told me they now had a new branch in Denver, where I live, and they would certainly be able to fit Daniel with a prosthesis...minus the travel time from Denver to Iowa.

I will not go into all that was involved in obtaining Daniel's passport except to say that the Ecuadorian ambassador in Washington, DC, and Pastor Rosa del Hierro made it happen rather quickly with minimal letters or phone contact from us. And it was *incredible* that I had never met his mom previously and she was still willing to send him with complete strangers who really did not speak much more Spanish than *hola,* and Daniel and his mom spoke *no English.* When we met at the Guayaquil Airport, Marilu/Mom was "great with child," and she and Daniel had made a six-hour bus ride through flooding El Niño rains. A trip that normally took two hours.

Once back on the plane, the crew was so enamored with Daniel and the event that they seated us in first class! On our flight back to Houston, I learned one innovative word in Spanish, *helado*, as Daniel was given water with ice in it...and he really did not want *helado* in his water! The Houston Airport was jam-packed, so during our long wait to get on a flight to Denver, I remember Daniel scouting around on the floor for minuscule pieces of paper. Then, he taught me a game with it... He always won.

After three months and being on three nightly newscasts, Daniel completed prosthetic "training." Our Bible study class gave him a left-handed guitar; the Neenans, our next-door neighbors, gave him guitar lessons, plus three elderly ladies from church gave him a speed course in English and a sendoff party—Daniel had charisma! Plus, he was returning home with much more than the solitary lunch bag holding trousers (that must have been his younger brother's) that accompanied him when coming.

I called the Ecuadorian missionaries to say Daniel's prosthetic fitting and training were complete, and we were returning with Daniel. However, the first three calls I placed, they did not answer. I thought I had inherited another son! On the fourth call, Pastor Rosa answered and said he would have to cross waist-deep water to get into his village...this was 1997/98 when El Niño ravaged the entire country. Could we wait a month?

During that month's wait, the Ecuadorian ambassador called me twice from DC. (As of yet, no one had clued him in that I am not Queen Elizabeth or heir to the Vanderbilt fortune, just Elizabeth.)

17

The ambassador wondered if we could help provide *road equipment* to help Ecuador with the devastation El Niño created. I was grieved and horrified hearing of mudslides that buried mountainside homes...and that the people only had their hands to dig with to save loved ones. I could not wrap my thoughts around the vision of horror created in my mind! *And unfortunately,* I certainly could not supply heavy road equipment.

With the second call from the ambassador, medical assistance was requested... If we could get a medical team as far as Miami, Ecuador's vice president would send his plane to pick us up... I did not say, "Are you kidding!" but certainly thought it.

Thanks to our mission director, Linda Olson, and pediatrician, Dr. Jim Shira, a team of nineteen was organized and headed for Ecuador with a stethoscope in one hand and a bag of collected medications in the other. Once we stepped off the plane in Guayaquil, "Queen Elizabeth treatment" began... Our plane was met by the Ecuadorian Military, who escorted us to and from our flight to Manabí Province, where we again stayed with the missionaries Pastors Rosa and Pedro del Hierro. In those four days, we "floated" to a different village each day and treated 1,700 very needy people.

An incredible mission, an *incredible* team; everyone worked beyond their strength in most unsavory conditions. Often, we used school desks that were moved outside for the "doctor's office" as they treated the unending extensive line of patients. I was totally awed by it *all*.

"And when he saw him, he had compassion. So, he went to him and bandaged his wounds...and took care of him."

(Luke 10:33b–34, NKJV)

CHAPTER 3

Clean Water

Upon our return to Colorado, Dr. Shira showed an extensive slide presentation to our Sunday morning Bible study. Appalled at the child mortality statistics, a friend posed the question, "Well, how could we help these people?" The response was evident and immediate, "*Clean* water." (At that time, we had been told over half of El Florón's children, two years and under, died from disease related to unsanitary water.)

Shortly after the presentation, Gordon Lewis resolved the question he previously asked regarding *clean water*. He suggested to me that we write a Rotary International clean water grant for their half-a-million-dollar 3M grant. "Gordon, I know *nothing* about writing a grant!"

"Well, you write the medical part, and I will do the business part...I'll get the forms." Gordon was undaunted by my comment; I am not even sure he heard my protest. "Well, okay...I will try," I *very* hesitantly replied... How insane was this notion! Little did I know that very humble Architect Gordon Lewis had written multiple grants for Rotary and drew up plans many times over the course of almost two years. Our Rotary grant writeup was returned a couple of times with suggestions. Then, we received a letter of apology from Rotary International stating that funding was tight; they were unable to grant us the full half-a-million-dollar amount. However, they were awarding us a grant of $495,000. I live in a different world...I could not believe an apology that was $5,000 short of a half a million dollars when we had zero to start with!

Gordon was the real champion on this project. He traveled to Ecuador with us on "buddy passes," which means that one is never sure when you will get on a flight, but the ticket price is impressive unless you spend multiple nights in a hotel because you repeatedly do not get on a flight. Gordon went to considerable effort in getting other US and Ecuadorian Rotary Clubs to support this project. Then "Amazing Gordon" also had a local Rotarian contact that he convinced to print 2,000 pictural booklets on hygiene and the mosquito cycle, which was included as part of my medical portion of the grant...to educate besides provide clean water.

"But be doers of the word, and not hearers only, deceiving yourselves."

(James 1:22, NKJV)

However, much to our surprise and dismay, the water piped into Florón was not potable; it was the same water trucks brought to dump into fifty-five-gallon containers for everyone in Florón to dip in and take to their homes. Del Stricker, one of our board members, picked up this challenging obstacle, dove into research, and discovered Steve Willner. (Steve reminds me of my grandpa in his bib overalls and flowing beard, which both cover incredible brilliance!) Steve not only built a reasonably priced water purification system but volunteered to come to Florón and install the system once it was shipped to Florón...this was months of grueling red tape. Ultimately, the US State Department did transport the entire system via a USAF cargo plane to Ecuador. That was sixteen years ago.

Today, you see an impressive mini water plant that my husband enlarged from the original. And, yes, frequent calls back to Steve in Denver. Richard retired from the airlines and always wanted to be an engineer. So he certainly waited on the Lord for this grand opportunity. He is Mr. Fixit or Mr. Improvise with what I would say is a very complicated system. He has trained four jobless Florón young men who now understand fair wages and benefits, including health care, vacations, and retirement.

CHAPTER 4

I Asked for $500

Not sure if I mentioned how all of this was originally financed... Some of you are aware from donating either financially, praying for Fundación "Yo Te Amo," Colorado, and/or contributing for many, many years. Initially, we began at our home with garage sales that got so out of hand that our church eventually agreed to hold them in the huge parking lot dotted with nine red and blue canopies.

Throughout the entire year, Richard filled and stuffed a donated rental storage unit since donations could never be contained in our home. I am talking about beautiful couches, lamps, clothes, and on and on. Then with gracious volunteers, Richard would transport *all* donations to the nine rented tent canopies at our church parking lot... It was a ton of work, but it not only filled the Yo Te Amo coffers but also was a great neighborhood/community outreach Friday and Saturday. Our congregation and friends were a tremendous help... Paul Corcoran and Amy Heavers would spend the night at the parking lot to guard the goods. Paul would fill his backpack with bricks (preparing for his annual summer mountain hike) as he cased the perimeter...what a guy! Oh yes, I do have a challenging time praying specifically...but for the very first garage sale at our home, I did secretly pray specifically... It was for $500. And we made $1,000.

"Be anxious for nothing; but in everything by prayer and supplication, with thanksgiving, Let your requests be known to God."

(Philippians 4:6, NKJV)

CHAPTER 5

Building a Hospital and Furnishing It?

When Gordon, Richard, and I were departing our final trip from Ecuador regarding water arrangements in Florón, Pastor Pedro timidly slipped a sheet of paper to me. On the paper was a basic computer printout of a two-story building floor plan and layout that he, in very few words in English, wanted to know if we could help with construction... I was floored! This was a highly intelligent man asking *me*! When I found my voice, I said possibly college students could come and help over the summer...and ultimately, that summer, I did "buddy pass" two college kids to Ecuador—Amy Heavers and Bob Thayer—to help build Pedro's hoped-for hospital.

Most unfortunately, Amy and Bob were confined *all summer* to the del Hierros' country hacienda since the police, doctors, and teachers of Ecuador had all gone on strike at precisely the same time. The country was extremely dangerous, with roads blocked with piles of burning tires and rioting everywhere. Back in the USA, I was fearfully nauseated for Bob and Amy's lives; repeatedly, I attempted to call the US ambassador in Guayaquil but never got through... Finally, Bob's mom, Patty, who was a close friend; our daughter Anna; and I went down to retrieve Amy and Bob; rioting had significantly settled down. Surprisingly, Amy did not return with us but stayed to teach English at the del Hierros' Christian high school in Montecristi... To say the least, I was extremely leery about leaving her behind. And unfortunately, not much was accomplished on the "hospital building" except stacks of adobe bricks that were delivered to the site.

When the building was completed by other mission teams and many people in the del Hierros' churches, I was asked the outlandish question if I could furnish it! (I know you are laughing if you are acquainted with me. *Furnish? Furnish* a hospital?)

However, *somewhere* along the way, I heard of "Project C.U.R.E." in the Denver area. (Actually, it was Amazing Gordon who told me about C.U.R.E.) As hospitals discard beds and equipment, Project C.U.R.E. takes the discarded items and supplies them to Developing Countries. We would be responsible for financing the shipping, but first, we needed to escort the CEO of Project C.U.R.E. to Ecuador to assess the building and make an inventory of all necessary medical equipment, furnishings, and supplies needed. CEO Dr. Doug Jackson was willing to go on a "buddy pass" but never will again.

Without incident, we initially boarded our flights and arrived in Ecuador; however, on our return home, it took us three days to board a flight in Quito for the States. Finally, there was a flight through Panama City where Richard and I, along with Dr. Jackson, were "bumped." Thus, we purchased a ticket for Dr. Jackson to Denver through Miami. I do not even remember how Richard and I eventually did get home... Aware of our bank account, we were prepared to swim.

To detail the cost and length of time the Project Cure shipment took to arrive in Florón would make you cry. The shipment was to go *directly* to the port city of Manta, which is about one hour from Florón, but instead, the shipment was offloaded in Guayaquil, where it was confiscated for six months...We (Pastor Pedro, his son James, and I) made weekly two-hour trips one way to Guayaquil. Each time we thought customs would surely release the shipment, only to be told of more necessary legal paperwork. When the glorious day did arrive, authorities informed us that we had to *pay* for the six months that customs "stored" the shipment they confiscated! Required payment was to the tune of $14,000! Fortunately, James's business finesse was able to have costs reduced to $8,000. (But where did we have $8,000 idly laying around?)

> *"Yet in all these things we are more than conquerors through Him who loved us."*
>
> (Romans 8:37, NKJV)

CHAPTER 6

The Benefit of Waiting

The two shipping containers in Guayaquil were loaded on semi-trucks escorted by machine-gun-toting guards. It was late at night, which did not improve the situation. Thus, upon the arrival at the Montecristi Church, the containers were secured and guarded for the night, only about forty-five minutes from El Florón and Buen Samaritano Clinic. The next morning was Sunday church services in Florón (which is next door to the clinic). As Pastor Rosa was preaching, she heard a rushing of water and intuitively screamed for her congregation to run next door to the clinic building since it had a second floor. The dam up the valley had fractured, and eight feet of water came careening down the valley. Rosa ensured that everyone was safe in the clinic...she, however, was not, and a firefighter pulled her out of the swirling water by grabbing her by locks of hair... Had the two-container shipment of clinic furnishings, equipment, and medical supplies been delivered the day prior, it would have all been lost in the flood.

"But let patience have its perfect work, that you may be perfect and complete, lacking nothing."

(James 1:4, NKJV)

CHAPTER 7

9/11 and a Medical Mission

In the forefront among my many "memory files" and yours also is the USA's horrific 9/11 catastrophe at New York's Twin Towers. Our medical mission team was to leave four days after that disastrous, evil event... Should we cancel the mission trip? Would anyone even come? Surprisingly, they did; even Lynette Conrad, physician's assistant, whom I had never even met until we all rendezvoused at the Houston Airport. Also expected to join the team was the well-seasoned world traveler MD who I had accompanied on medical missions in the jungle of Belize and who had come on that first "El Niño" medical mission. Well, he *said* he was flying; then, he said he would drive to Houston instead of fly, and finally, he said his family refused to let him come; I understood but was majorly disappointed. That meant PA Conrad was left holding the bag as our only practitioner...gulp! Looking back, Lynette had folded up wings and a halo that was noticed by all. Coming from Nevada, soft-spoken, gentle Lynette had left behind her husband and two small children.

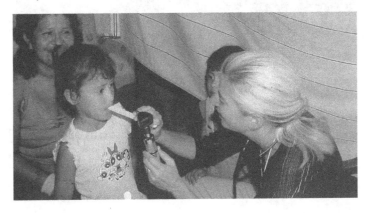

Surely, divine intervention brought her presence to this team. Long lines of impoverished patients kept us distracted from the destruction that we left behind in our beloved country. However, missionary Rosa del Hierro touched our hearts when she had us begin the first day of clinic by the team sitting in the church as the school children marched in displaying the American flag, half mast, as our national anthem loudly flowed out of a scratchy tape recorder. Each of our team was deeply moved and teary and felt united with our new Ecuadorian friends, the multitudes waiting to be seen, and the challenging task at hand.

"...there is a friend who sticks closer than a brother."
(Proverbs 18:24b, NKJV)

I am not sure if it was this mission trip or the one after when a prominent lady brought a man to our medical clinic. Esenerio was from the jungle. I had met Gloria Sandoval during the Rotary 3M Water Project; her husband was a Rotarian and president of a Manta bank. Gloria's compassionate heart brought Esenerio, who was in his early forties and had been bedridden from extreme arthritis for the past two years. His sons carried him in a human sling draped from a thick bamboo pole.

Gloria said if I could obtain two prosthetic hips in the US, she could have the surgery done in Quito, where her brother-in-law was the head cardiologist. At that moment, I did not have two prosthetic hips in my pocket...I did not even have one or know where to purchase them or have them donated. But I said I would try. (I was not even sure what to "try"!) I do not honestly remember how I eventually came upon the prosthetic hips but what I do remember is that Esenerio did have the surgery in Quito and that he and his two new hips returned home on the bus. The ride was about a six-hour trip from Quito to his jungle home. This information was from Gloria, who wanted herself, Richard, and I to visit Esenerio and his family in the jungle. It was monsoon season, so Gloria's Mercedes engine and tires ultimately refused to tackle any more deep, gooey clay mud. Thus, we trekked, slipping and sliding the last couple of "American blocks" through the jungle. And there was Esenerio with his wife wildly waving from their open-air picture window.

His joy was that he could now dance! (And to this day, I cannot figure out how he ever made that six-hour bus ride home just days after surgery...amazing!) Surprisingly, months later, one Sunday, he attended the Florón Church to thank me again and show me again how his newly gained hips could dance...and dance he did!

CHAPTER 8

Juliana

Physical anomalies should be restricted from the impoverished, but then I would never have known the delight of my friend Juliana. She now goes by her middle name, "Vanessa." In Florón, both adults and children make this switch between their first and middle name. I think initially, they are known by their middle name and later decide to go by their first name or vice versa. (This *totally* confuses me!) Anyway, I will stick to "Juliana," who was born with a three-chambered heart (normal is four) and the two major vessels leading into the heart transposed.

Rosa introduced me to her mom, Francesca, who was cradling her infant in her arms and facially expressing deep concern as only a mother can. I contacted my affluent friend, Gloria, who said she could arrange an appointment for Juliana with her brother-in-law, who is a cardiologist in Quito.

A week later, close to midnight, Francesca, Fernando, little Juliana, and I boarded a bus for the eight-hour trip to Quito. About three hours into the trip, the bus pulled over to the roadside, stopped, and on stomped six grey uniformed men toting machine guns. We were all told to disembark; women in one line, men in the other. As Francesca cradled a bundled-up Juliana in her arms, the one *hombre* thrust his hand between the bundle and her breasts (I would have slapped him if he didn't have that machine gun strapped to his chest). No words were spoken, but when all women were physically scanned, we were motioned to get back on the bus. As I sat on my seat, my overactive imagination was sure the men would be shot... they were out there at least twenty minutes before they returned to the bus. Not a word was spoken—I was aghast—and away we went on the rough, winding roads to Quito.

We arrived in Quito at about 8 a.m. I am *not* a night person, and I was pretty much comatose; rough roads prevented sleep or even dozing. Rosa had arranged for her nephew to pick us up. My charges were taken to a hotel, and I was taken to Rosa's sister, where I was put to bed in the most comfortable bed I can remember. I was not comfortable with "abandoning" Francesca, Fernando, and little Juliana to a hotel but was too weary to challenge the arrangements.

Dr. Sandoval was a distinguished professional man. I thanked him multiple times for seeing us; he shared how, when young, he had been in an airplane crash and been the only survivor. He said he knew he survived for a definite purpose. After exams, X-rays (I think it was), and reading her past report, he commented that he had seen many of these children live into their twenties. A heart transplant was slim to none in Ecuador. (When I returned home, I did contact a friend whose brother was a cardiologist at Yale University. The resolve was that finding a match from another country was next to impossible, and Juliana and her mom would have to stay in the US post-surgery at least a year after to watch for rejection of the new heart...not to mention the strain of being away from her culture, family, and speaking no English. I had never thought of all that and recalled how terrified Francesca was of being in Quito for the first time. I had found Fernando scurrying down the hotel hall late at night, and he said Francesca had a migraine headache. I dropped the idea of heart transplant in the US.)

Years have gone by, and I continue to see Juliana often, and on her birthday, we annually go to a movie, have popcorn, and eat at the food court at the Portoviejo Mall.

She (and always included is her niece "Meiby"—pronounced "maybe"—who is younger only by a couple of years) and Meiby come back to our apartment for snacks... They love to do my dishes and use our bathroom...and snoop around our little apartment. What incredible joy for me!

I know Juliana has been to the Children's Hospital in Guayaquil. At one point, they wanted to do a procedure on her, but she told her parents, "No, I just want to live for whatever time I have left and have a computer and play the piano." She graduated from high school this past year. And now she is at the university and taking piano lessons. And someone donated a keyboard to "Yo Te Amo" that we gave to Juliana. She now has a cell phone and WhatsApp. We text every couple of weeks...and she is texting in perfect English, which she is also taking at the university. She also was proud to send me a picture of her recent baptism with the comment, "...everything is better if it goes hand in hand with God..." Our friendship is one of God's many gifts to me.

Besides concerns for Juliana, Francesca pleadingly asked me to visit their son, Miguel, in the hospital, where he receives dialysis twice a week. I did visit, and there were patients lined up in beds receiving dialysis. You would not believe how prevalent this is... Someone should do a study on why diabetes and kidney disease cases are so high in this area. Surprisingly, Miguel is married, has a child, and is finishing his education at the government's free university. Two years prior, Francesca had asked us if they could borrow a mattress for Miguel, and we delivered one to their home in Florón 8. I wondered what the rest of the family slept on. I have never been invited into the home.

> "Open your mouth, judge righteously, And plead the
> cause of the poor and needy."
>
> (Proverbs 31:9, NKJV)

CHAPTER 9

Consuelo

Ultimately, smaller mission groups were taken to Guayaquil, Ecuador, via "buddy passes," thanks to Continental Airlines and my husband. The flight makes a brief stop in Quito and continues to Guayaquil. This particular time certain team members were told to disembark the aircraft... Again, our destination was Guayaquil, *not* Quito. My husband accompanied us on this trip, and when they started to call team members names...Richard knew that if the plane did not take off immediately, the airline would be fined and grounded to overnight in Quito... Thus, the ethical pilot that he was, he did not challenge the flight attendant and finally stood up and signaled all the team to disembark the plane... I was horrified! It was midnight! Where were we going to go? And we had no funds for this unexpected "side trip"! Richard and I stood on the tarmac with looks of horrified disbelief at each other, with our team surrounding us as we all watched the big "silver bird" lumber down the runway and then devoured by the night.

Finally, we all turned and slowly ambled into the terminal with our fledgling team, some individuals whom we had just met earlier that day in Houston. Once inside, Richard and my eyes locked, and we tried not to divulge in our gaze; this was a major mess! Then, out of nowhere, a young woman approached and said in perfect English, "My friend's parents have room for you but only your group." (Others not on our team were also taken off the flight.) Numbly, robotically, we nodded, and all followed her... (But I then recalled months earlier, Denver missionaries in Quito went for a Sunday drive in the Andean

Mountains and were forced off the road, and the husband was shot and killed.) As we piled into a pickup truck and taxis and then drove down a dark, uninhabited road, my overactive mind recalled that past tragedy and thought, *They are going to kill us. Why did we ever go with these complete strangers? We are responsible for this team!*

A huge metal door slowly, electronically opened to a perky, friendly lady who escorted us to lovely, traditionally decorated Ecuadorian *cabañas*. As I shivered and snuggled way down under the covers that night, my Bible had this final verse for that day:

> *"[I] will go with you; and I will give you rest."*
> (Exodus 33:14, NIV)

...And He did.

In the morning, we were greeted by bright sunlight, a hillside home with beautifully manicured landscape...and that same lady, who reintroduced herself as "Consuelo," her husband, Patricio, and daughter, Camila. This lovely home was decorated with multiple works of art in various mediums...Consuelo's father had been an artist and architect. In high school, she had been an exchange student to the state of Washington; thus, she had excellent English and currently taught English to Ecuadorian businessmen traveling to the US. Breakfast was huge, delicious, and *so* welcomed. (If our team sensed our complete distress when we were taken off the plane the previous night, we hoped we had been redeemed in their eyes by God's mercy.) Richard and I will *never* forget that entire escapade...

I will try to not belabor that situation but mention that from that single event, Consuelo and Patricio have not only continued to host our teams but have accompanied us and our mission teams to

Florón, where Consuelo interprets and always keeps us laughing...
while Patricio gives Richard much appreciated male support around
the clinic. There are no words to describe what their friendship has
meant to our family and us. Our daughter lived with them for her
Spanish immersion, and Consuelo affectionately calls herself "Anna's
Ecuadorian mom."

"Giving thanks always for all the things to God the
Father in the name of our Lord Jesus Christ,..."
(Ephesians 5:20, NKJV)

CHAPTER 10

I'm a Nurse—Not an Administrator

During the first few years of the clinic being open, staff changes were like a revolving door. I was aware—or thought I was—that this was *not* the USA. I did not forget my lowered expectations needed to be heavily imprinted with "patience" and "temperance" stamped on each employee's forehead. And yes, by now, Rosa and Pedro had asked me to administrate the clinic.

I can honestly say I was not flattered but aghast; firmly honest, I assured them, "I don't know anything about administrating a clinic." However, it was their sincerity, and, by now, I better understood they went into severely impoverished communities that *no one else* would dare to set foot in, let alone to start a church, much less a school in such ghastly, impoverished, and dangerous areas. I no longer had reason to question their motives...just myself and God Himself. But who was I? Certainly, no one special, but I had to admit to myself *I was someone that continually was supplied with "someone else" that did have the knowledge or know-how that I did not possess.* For example, Pastor Pedro thought the "hospital" could be arranged a certain way. (And initially, I thought he had hospital expertise, and I did not question anything he directed.) Then, one day Dr. Pedro Mendoza, whom I had met from the Rotary 3M Water Project, unexpectedly visited me at Buen Samaritano... He said patients *could not enter* by the entrance that directly opened to the upstairs second floor as we had planned... patients and family members were curious and would go upstairs... Thus, the patient entrance was changed to the far end of the clinic building. Dr. Mendoza also informed me that we could not open as a "hospital"... We first needed to begin as an *asistencial* (Spanish), which we Americans would call a "clinic"... Contrastingly, Rosa and Pedro said I did not even need to have it licensed. *None* of their schools were licensed, and *many* children in poverty were brought to Jesus Christ—their evangelistic purpose. However, I recalled a verse in Scripture that addressed being a foreigner, who I was, and obeying the laws of the land. Thus, if I was going to administrate an *asistencial* or clinic, then I *must* work under the laws of Ecuador.

> *"Let every soul be subject to the governing authorities."*
>
> (Romans 13:1, NKJV)

Dr. Mendoza was a medical and administrative mentor I am most thankful for; he later—unknowingly—answered my need for an orthopedic surgeon.

As I continued to work toward licensure, Dra. Lorena Mejia, whom I had never met, visited Buen Samaritano and announced that she would sign for us to be licensed as an *asistencial*; Dra. Mejia observed that we met standard requirements. Dra. Mejia became a friend and later did *gratis* surgery for our nurse assistant with uterine cancer. On another occasion, Dr. Mejia invited me to lunch out of her deep concern for our night guard...as you will later read.

"And my God will meet all your needs..."
(Philippians 4:19, NIV)

What can I say except the Holy Spirit within guided and directed my path as God supplied *all* my needs...including multiple people with expertise that I did not possess. His continual protection surrounded these twenty-five years. I recall multiple instances when my husband and I or our staff's lives were in life-threatening situations...

*"Yea, though I walk through the valley of the shadow
of death, I will fear no evil; For You are with me..."*

(Psalm 23:4, NKJV)

One rather humorous note but not to make sport of this dear young man—one evening, the night guard came to me and reported that the previous night someone had come over the eight-foot wall that surrounded the clinic compound. Our night guard ran next door to get Pastor Gruezo. I asked him if he could describe this person. In sincere earnest, he replied, "Sure, it was my cousin!" The following day he came to diligently report to me that he went to his cousin's home and verbally threatened, "Do not ever do that again; I could lose my job!" Laughing would certainly have been inappropriate, but inwardly, I could hardly contain myself; I patted him on the back and thanked him for taking care of the matter.

CHAPTER 11

Flori

(L-R) Flori, Candy—Peacemaker Ministries, Consuelo.

Probably you would have to meet Lawyer Flori Zambrano to understand integrity and humility encapsulated in one small person who is forced to read with a magnifying device because of an ocular deformity. My acquaintance to this miraculous little lady goes back to 2014. I was having more than a challenge trying to find a physician to function as the medical director of the clinic. At the time, I was staying in a lovely apartment at the top of James and Ximena del Hierro's home in Manta; Pastors Rosa and Pedro del Hierro lived in the other apartment. Previously, they introduced me to a very classy friend who was a little "manic" and married to a brilliant man who would make me insane, both very genial people. Anyway, she insisted

I talk to her pastor, who she thought could assist me with a physician. Thus, she drove me from Manta to Portoviejo—a forty-five-minute, hair-raising "adventuresome ride." The pastor was very cordial but spoke no English...and my Spanish—well, I was too embarrassed to even try, but I did smile and nod frequently. The encounter was pleasant and brief. He suggested I tour the church's medical clinic a half-block away. To describe this area, I can say the church and the medical clinic were definitely a few "steps above" economically than the poverty in Florón.

Their clinic administrator at that time was Flori, a lawyer who had been an exchange student to Greeley, Colorado, which is an hour's drive from Denver. Flori was fluent in English, and that is how this incredible friendship began...

Flori has written our clinic contracts, directed us on Ecuadorian law regarding benefits, legal salary increases, and so forth, plus advised us on "precarious situations" such as an accident where I was briefly incarcerated (Our kids enjoy flaunting that they never did that!); all of which could fill a book in and of itself...but more importantly than the plethora of various legal matters, Flori Zambrano has been a friend who has wisely shepherded us as one Christian to another... The legal successes of Buen Samaritano can be traced directly to the wise guidance and kindness of Flori.

> *"Behold! My Servant whom I uphold, My Elect One*
> *in whom My soul delights! I have put My Spirit upon*
> *Him [her]; He will bring forth justice to the Gentiles."*
>
> (Isaiah 42:1, NKJV)

CHAPTER 12

Dr. Randi

One Sunday morning, I scurried into Bible study...late again. Richard was trying to inconspicuously mouth something to me without turning his head. I was not catching on...then, he held up a business card and pointed to the middle of his chest, indicating the couple was sitting behind us. I finally got it!

As soon as class was over, I immediately turned and faced a handsome young couple—Randi was an Ob/Gyn MD, and Charlie was a lawyer. They said the magic words again, "If you ever need help..." "Really." I thought I reeked of needing help! Not only did they help me try to test out a secondhand ultrasound on Charlie's pregnant secretary, but Randi was interested in coming to Ecuador.

Come she did! Multiple times, and accompanied by a new microscope for our laboratory, she trained Dra. Silvia in collecting Papanikolaou specimens...which the clinic then began to offer to patients. But Dr. Randi did not stop there. She gathered colleagues from various medical specialties to join our medical missions, which now were an annual event. Dr. Randi even convinced her husband to come on one trip to help build a jungle gym and swing set that resided in the front clinic yard. On that same trip, her sister-in-law (a former Fox news writer) and a friend who filmed promo videos for Promise Keepers came to put together a promotional video for FYTA... This still can be seen on our web page. They put in *multiple* man-hours to produce this. And at a later time, Dr.McVay's daughter, Abby, came and did a fun Vacation Bible School for all the local kids...

The McVays' contribution to the clinic is beyond words...

"I will bless those who bless you..."
(Genesis 12:3a, NKJV)

Chapter 13

And Then There Was Dr. Claire

Did you ever mentally judge someone in your mind, not verbally but a passing thought? And later discover you were 100 percent wrong! Very, very humbling.

Always, I have been thrilled and astounded when someone actually asks to visit Florón and help in any way they can. And so it was that Dr. Claire Guam chose to come on her three-week pediatric residency rotation. Dr. Claire was one of these ladies that could zoom out of her bedroom five minutes before staff devotions, arrive on time, and look terrific! Dr. Claire said she was willing to help in any *way* she could. (*Never* say that to Richard.) He had Dr. Claire spreading/raking a new pile of gravel that had just been delivered. I thought that was a bit much, but Claire said,

"Oh, I love yard work." Beyond "yard work," Dr. Claire assisted in seeing patients at the clinic and then held a special clinic at outlying churches that were medically underserved. Children adored this perky, outgoing doctor and did not resist exams, which they seemed to enjoy.

Usually, patients come in the morning when it is cooler. Afternoons are quieter, and I would notice Dr. Claire engrossed in her iPad and strolling about the compound... I confess my thoughts were not positive...but not that she should be raking gravel! But how could she spend that much time on her iPad? As I discovered at the end of Dr. Claire's three weeks, she had been making a video on clean water and used Carlos, one of the water technicians, to share in Spanish the desperate need for clean water. The video was impressively arranged and was most informative. Me? Yes, I was ashamed of how I had jumped to conclusions. Today, Dr. Claire continues her medical education in international diseases. We were profoundly blessed with her two visits to Buen Samaritano Clinic in Florón.

> *"I will instruct you and teach you in the way you*
> *should go; I will guide you with My Eye."*
>
> (Psalm 32:8, NKJV)

CHAPTER 14

"Mom, What Should I Do About This?"

Our second physician or medical director was introduced to me by Pastor Pedro del Hierro. (Our first physician was asked to leave after concerning obvious personal issues.) Dr. Parralles was a professor of biology and anatomy and a surgeon by trade. I asked Pastor Pedro to sit in on the interview in case I got "stuck" with my not-so-perfect Spanish. Dr. Parralles was an exceedingly kind and gentle man. There was no doubt of his capability as a surgeon. During the interview, I asked him if he had a personal relationship with Jesus; he sat and pondered the question for what seemed like an exceptionally long time. I was not sure if it was my poor command of the language or the question itself. Finally, he slowly and perplexed shook his head and quietly said he did not think so. Out of respect, I asked Pastor Pedro to explain and lead him to Jesus. This remains a precious memory for me.

Here I must comment that an excellent surgeon is not necessarily a capable medical director. This was verified by our youngest daughter (an RN at that time). Anna had asked my husband and I if she could work as a volunteer nurse in the clinic for six months so we could focus more on fundraising at home in Colorado. Prior to beginning work at the clinic, Anna was willing for the first month to do Spanish immersion with Consuelo in Quito. (Unlike her mother, Anna is quick to pick up a language and had had four years of German.)

And in retrospect, Anna herself would have been an excellent administrator. Her frequent phone calls from the clinic to me in Colorado went like this: "Mom, Dr. Parralles is sleeping in his office; what do you want me to do?" "Mom, Dr. Parralles has been out watching the guys play soccer for two hours; what do you want me to do?"

We *loved* this guy, and it was not like he was neglecting patients...there just were not any patients. However, administrating a clinic—especially a new facility—spans much farther than attending patients. (It means chasing to get them!)

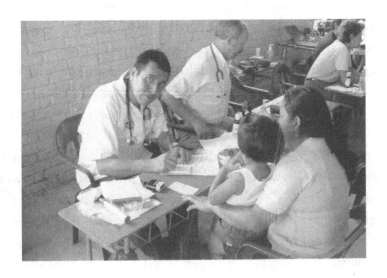

Thus, when we returned to Florón with a medical mission team, I knew what I had to do; I was painfully grieved. These are times I tell myself that if Jesus could return, I would be freed of this unsavory task. After I introduced the mission team to the staff, I settled the team in their second-floor "hospital rooms." I sat down in Dr. Parralles' office for "the chat." But before I mustered up the courage to initiate that unsavory conversation, he said he was deeply sorry that he could not continue working at the clinic. He relayed that he took three different busses to arrive at Buen Samaritano each morning, and he had bad varicose veins... He just could not continue... I tried to be empathetic, but the truth was I was internally ecstatic! I still feel the relief as I peck away at the keys and share that uncomfortable event.

However, I *cannot* let Dr. Parralles go from these pages quite yet. I hope I have painted what a celebrated individual and surgeon he was. A few years after Dr. Parallels left Buen Samaritano, Pastor Gruezo came to me in the strictest confidence. There was a new couple in church; both had confirmed AIDS. Before coming to Christ, they did not know there was anything wrong with sleeping with various partners; they certainly did now, *and* even of more concern, she was pregnant. Pastor Rosa was totally *against* Dr. Parralles delivering the baby; Dr. Parallels was totally *for* delivering the baby and did so to a healthy baby boy. USA's Dr. Randi McVay provided the medicine for the baby's first six months so the virus would not harm the baby. Fast-forwarding to a few years even later, the same lady had a breast mass, and it was Dr. Parralles who performed—*without question*—the biopsy. He is one of my heroes of impeccable integrity; while he was still working with us, he was so proud to be working in the clinic that he invited the staff over to his home in Manta to meet his wife. Sadly, he died rather young of a heart attack… I am honored to know Dr. Parralles and look forward to seeing this dear Christian man again.

> *"The righteous shall flourish like a palm tree, He shall grow like a cedar in Lebanon."*
>
> (Psalm 92:12, NKJV)

Chapter 15

You Want to Do What!

Prior to our daughter Anna departing to work in Buen Samaritano Clinic, you may recall Amy, who went to help "build" the clinic. Ultimately, Amy stayed to teach English for a time and then returned to Colorado. She now was offering to also work in the clinic after Anna's six months ended. Frankly, we told her that we were unable to pay a salary, only provide "a roof over her head." Her response was like Anna's, "I have saved up for a year and sold my car to my sister and subleased my apartment to her. So how about a penny a month to keep you honest?" These are moments when you wonder if you went to heaven or suspiciously think, *What is the catch?*

Amy's year is a wonderfully long story... I will not go into all the precious and beneficial events of also having Amy at the clinic. But I want to share two noteworthy events during that year. The first being a little boy named Elias...not exactly an orphan but "sort of." He and two older brothers lived with their grandmother, who I was told locked them in her "on stilts shack" at night while she went on to other evening events. Amy and dear Albita, clinic assistant, took Elias under their wing and purchased a white shirt and navy trousers and a *waaaay* too big belt to hold his trousers up and a second pair of used shoes so he could attend the church's school.

Elias would come every morning, and elderly Albita would scrub him down outside with the garden hose and dress him. (Once, when I was there, I said, "This kid has no underwear on!" Yes! I am a typical American... Not sure if any other kids did either.)

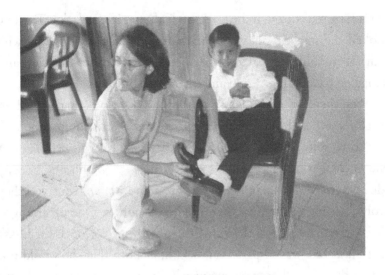

Anyway, Elias seemed pretty content with the program since Amy or Albita also fed him breakfast. When the clinic's annual dental program started for the church's school kids, it was noticed that Elias had a tooth that grew sideways and "dug" a good-sized gaping hole in his cheek. The tooth was extracted, and we got him on antibiotics three times a day... I could give two doses when the clinic was open, but I needed to go to his "home" to give the third dose. Pastor Gruezo said that it was too dangerous for me to go alone even though it was only two short blocks away from the clinic. So Pastor Gruezo, his son, and I ambled over to the house on stilts. I climbed a half-broken-down, rickety ladder to get to the "front door." Since there were no lights, I was more than a little scared to open the door, even with Pastor Gruezo and Eduardo standing there. I knocked, and as I opened the door, there were the three siblings on a filthy mattress curled up like sleeping puppies. Ugh! Which one was Elias? Bodies were all swirled together. I do not know how else to describe it. But I gently "rutted" through the three-body masses in the dark... This one looked the smallest body and head...it was a very sleepy Elias who half sat up and slurped the liquid antibiotic without question and snuggled back into position among his two brothers.

Yes, there are multiple tales with Elias. One was that he had no birth record, so he could never get credit for attending school. So I tried to solve that by taking his adult uncle to register Elias, but the uncle was not acceptable to authorities... "No, no one has any idea where Mom is...he lives with his grandmother." But yes, they would accept verification from the grandmother. One prearranged day, Grandma came to the clinic to go with me to vouch for Elias's birthdate. She was so paranoid, drunk, or both that she would not get in the car and accused me of who knows what. Eventually, we were warned about giving little Elias breakfast and getting him ready and sending him to school... Unbelievably, we could be charged with owing money to Grandma. Children could be "rented." To our sadness, Elias eventually disappeared. Later, Amy saw him in the business district of Portoviejo; he was with an older man... Amy thought Elias was being used to steal, and he did not acknowledge Amy... Really, no point in continuing except to say Amy and Albita were saints planted somewhere in Elias's chaotic life.

If you can, recall the beautiful biblical story of Jacob and Rachel. If not, know his love for her had him working seven years for her father to claim her hand in marriage. (However, he got tricked by his uncle and first betrothed her older sister Leah and then had to work seven more years for Rachel.)

Anyway, by this time, Amy had worked in Ecuador on and off for a total of almost seven years. During her stint as an English teacher that first time in Ecuador, one of her students, Cleofe, had more than a "crush" on her. Once she returned to the United States, Cleofe would give me letters to deliver to her. The serious young man was passionate and not hampered by distance. Amy, on the other hand, was just not into romance; she was practical and sought a spiritual path that did not include Cleofe. Once, when he gave me a letter to transport, he dramatically said in his best English, "Amy...she will not have me!" It was so unlike this serious young man that I almost burst out laughing. But I did ache for this handsome young man who led music in church. (The thought honestly crossed my mind, *Well, I still have one daughter remaining. And she does not have "weak eyes" like Leah in the Bible.* My daughters would see no humor in this.)

Almost seven years passed when Amy returned to work in Buen Samaritano Clinic. Eventually, Cleofe discovered that Amy was back in Ecuador working at the clinic, which was about forty-five minutes away from his home in Montecristi. He called and asked if he could see her. "No, the Engkjers have strict rules, and no one can be in the clinic after it closes," Amy responded.

Even though Cleofe now did have another girlfriend, he was not deterred. "How about if we meet at the mall?"

"No. You have a girlfriend."

"Well, I will bring her along." The threesome met at the mall, and according to Amy, they just walked around the mall... Really, there is no other "hang out" for teens in all of Portoviejo.

And Cleofe's love seemed to build in "momentum." "Could we meet again in the park by the mall?"

"No, you have a girlfriend."

"I'll get rid of her."

"No, you have to talk to Pastor Pedro." (Are you joking! This is hilarious. They were both in their late twenties.)

However, Cleofe *did* ask Pastor Pedro! My heart did ache for the other girlfriend; I bet her mom had the wedding all planned.

Amy and Cleofe now live nearby us in Colorado...

They have two beautiful children; Amy is the chairlady of our board, and Cleofe is our computer whiz who is an IT specialist with Cherry Creek School District and now an elder and choir leader in a large church with many Hispanic people that we all attend. Amy has maintained a very close relationship with our clinic director, Dra. Silvia...What can I say except that His plan can be very surprising and full of twists and turns!

Oh, yes...Cleofe and his construction manager, brother-in-law, Jason, both accompanied Richard to Ecuador to build the large addition to the water purification building. Upon their return, Jason said Richard made great egg, ham, cheese, and mayo sandwiches that they ate *every day*...except once they had tuna. It is called *endurance*.

CHAPTER 16

"Elizabeth, What Are You Going to Do About This?"

There are many significant "happenings" with each mission trip; I will never get to them all. But one occurred with a nurse practitioner, Kay Alsum, who wanted me to see the grossly deformed foot of little María Angélica, who was five at the time. Unlike confident Daniel, this deformity pretty much made little María Angélica an outcast. Kay wanted to know what we could do about this.

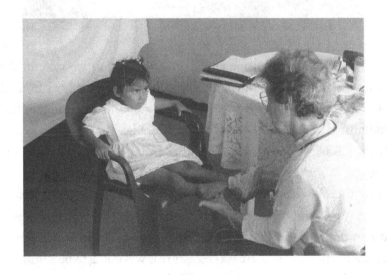

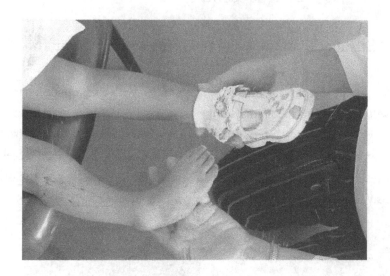

I took the child's name and that of the pastor; we were in the dusty, very dirty village of Carnitas, which was about an hour from El Florón. María Angélica lived with her grandmother; her mother had committed suicide, and her dad was an alcoholic, nowhere to be found. Grandmother's house was high on stilts, and their pigs lived under the bottom. What was I going to do about this! What was I going to do about this...? What was I going to do about this! I had *no earthly idea!*

A week went by; the team returned to the US, and I was attempting to improve the clinic's organization. (In Spanish, "clinic" means hospital...and there was *no way* this was going to be a hospital even if this is what Pastors Rosa and Pedro had had in mind.) Anyway, I was trying to figure out what mess needed to be organized when Dr. Pedro Mendoza drove in. (Very unusual at that time. No one set foot in Florón without a bodyguard.) Dr. Mendoza had another physician with him. He introduced him as Dr. Cristóbal Alban. You recall we had met Dr. Mendoza with the Rotary Water Project. Neither of these two dignified doctors really spoke English, but Dr. Mendoza did relay that Dr. Alban was an orthopedic surgeon in case I ever needed one. *In case I ever need one?* I just burst into tears... No telling what went through these men's thoughts at that moment. Once I "composed myself," I told them that we had a five-year-old girl in Carnitas that had a severe club foot...would there be any possibility that Dr. Alban could help her? I understood him to say it would be no problem.

However, getting María Angélica to the surgical table ended up being a seemingly insurmountable challenge...with great difficulty, her alcoholic father was finally located, but he refused to give permission for the surgery. I was astounded and, yes, angry. Surgery was postponed for three days, and finally, María's father was convinced to give permission for surgery. I watched the surgery and stayed with María Angélica, who pathetically whiningly cried nonstop. When I could take no more of her wailing, I hesitantly called Dr. Alban... He said "they" (meaning impoverished people) have not experienced pain of this nature; no extra meds were ordered. (*This is certainly not the USA*, I regretfully thought.) I did see María a year or so later when her grandmother proudly brought her to the clinic to see me... She and Grandma were all smiles as she walked in with one shoe elevated and walked close to normal. Now, she is a beautiful young lady who still lives with Grandma in a house above the pigs...

She and loving Grandma unknowingly blessed my life, even now. For me, Dr. Alban entering my life...my desperate need and that of Maria Angélica...remain as God's provision of one of *many* unseen modern-day miracles in El Florón, Ecuador, and around the world.

"Through the Lord's mercies we are not consumed,
Because his compassions fail not."

(Lamentations 3:22, NKJV)

Chapter 17

My Deepest Valley

Pepe and Mayra were youth pastors at the church next to the clinic. Mayra was also a teacher with Compassion International. Pepe, the clinic's night guard, was a handsome jock that drew many to the youth group... Once he and Mayra took over youth ministry, the number of attendees went from eight to eighty. I recall he and Mayra came to show me the Mother's Day video they made with each youth interviewed and wishing their mom a happy Mother's Day. It was—pardon me—hilarious! These big, strapping brutes of guys shyly wishing their mom "Happy Mother's Day" on video. Moms were invited to the church for games with their offspring and to watch the video. This was *most* impressive.

My deepest valley—though I was not aware of it at the time—was Pepe. It began with a call at our home in Colorado; our night guard was thought to have appendicitis. Yes, of course, he should have the surgery, and we would pay the cost.

It seemed to take forever for the pathology report to return. *For heaven's sake, what* is *the problem!* I do get upset when I see impoverished people treated like they do not matter. And so we returned to Ecuador. What was thought to be a simple appendicitis was not; it was an exceedingly rare tumor—a *neuroendocrine mass.* Dr. Lorena Mejia invited Amy and me to her home for lunch. (Dr. Mejia was a special friend who, you may remember, had volunteered to sign for the clinic when seeking licensure.) Now she very pointedly wanted me aware of the gravity of Pepe's diagnosis... She strongly advised me to take Pepe to the United States if possible. At that time, our daughter was in graduate school at Johns Hopkins University... She reaffirmed the rarity of a neuroendocrine tumor not only in the United States but around the world... Two physicians (one a radiologist and one the medical director for the western divisions of Kaiser Hospitals) in our koinonia again reaffirmed the rarity of this type of tumor.

Pepe had the best surgeon, whom I requested; I knew his father—a very well-respected pediatrician whose son held the same attributes. Pepe's dad, Oscar, wanted Richard to go into surgery and film the operation... He and many had fervently been praying; Oscar *was sure* there would be no tumor once the surgery was performed. Sadly and regrettably, this was not the case. I remember Oscar's fist pounding the hospital wall immediately following the surgeon's unwelcomed findings. We were all numb, disheartened...no, grieved beyond words.

Oscar had this old jalopy of a pickup truck that sputtered, blew black smoke, and did not always arrive at the intended destination, so we had volunteered to bring Pepe home from the hospital when the time came. I clearly remember that day; many from the youth group were at the clinic to welcome home their "hero." But they were not prepared to see Pepe assisted from the car by Pastor Meza and Hermano Fabricio and pretty much drag him since he was heavily medicated and his feet refused to cooperate as they took him into the clinic and up to the second-floor room, which we had prepared and would be his home for the next several weeks.

A week or so passed, and a touching scene occurred that is engraved in my mind as if it were yesterday. Whispering, whispering... "Hermana Elizabeth, please open the back gate to the clinic." And in silently crept about thirty loving people, each holding a lit candle. "Hermana, can you bring Pepe to the window?" Mayra and I helped Pepe to the window. And quietly, they sang two of his favorite songs and then silently departed with candles glowing. Can human love go any deeper than this?

Yes.

> *"...but there is a friend that sticks closer than a*
> *brother"*
>
> (Proverbs 18:24b, NIV)

This was a precious mountain top moment as Pepe and we slid down the other side of that mountain.

I recall this one Sunday after church; Mayra's mom, Pastor Carmen, came to me and said Mayra was so depressed and crying... She thought she might be pregnant, but time told her she was not. They had wanted children so desperately...would I talk to Mayra, please? Amazing to me was that Pepe was nineteen and Mayra was fifteen when they married. Once, I had asked Mayra why her mom had ever let her marry so young... She said, "My mom knew I really loved Pepe." And she did.

But after nine years of marriage, they were not blessed with children. My heart ached for them, especially at that moment.

Pepe did start on the "big guns" of chemotherapy; all medical people at Solca (originally a cancer hospital started by a Dr. Solca) were aware of the virulency of this vicious tumor. If Pepe continued the chemo, the hospital would supply him with the necessary analgesia for pain. But when Pepe said, "No more nausea and vomiting," the hospital "deleted him as a patient" from their patient roster. No more analgesia, no more anything. One afternoon, I remember taking him to the ER at Solca for severe dental pain. We waited in the ER for three hours. When he was finally examined, no meds were given. I was furious—if you do not play their experimental treatment game, you lose. You are dropped from their radar and responsibility... "God, do You know how much I need You now? Watching him suffer is more than I can bare... He is so young...could not it be me? My life has been blessed by You. I am ready. Please, I am *begging* You." Today, as I document this, my tears flow freely as I could not allow then. And I can thank God for allowing me to walk through that time with Pepe, Mayra, and their families.

What amazed me then was Mayra... As handsome Pepe declined (flaccid muscle tone, almost unrecognizable)...Mayra never seemed to see his decline, and he remained her handsome husband whom she married at fifteen and he nineteen. They had been married nine years. Yes, she really did intensely love Pepe.

Once, I phoned an on-call MD to the house for Pepe's excruciating pain. He was truly kind but explained the reality of no longer being a patient at Solca Hospital, i.e., no responsibility or pain meds... I did not want to hear it... I tried begging pain meds from the pharmacy that I previously used... I think I got tramadol a couple of times, which really was an inadequate joke for the pain Pepe was experiencing. I remember one morning, Richard was sitting on our little second-floor four-by-five-feet apartment patio... He called to me, "Liz, you better get over there...I hear Pepe screaming."

By this time, he and Mayra had moved from the second floor of the clinic over to his parents' home, about one hundred yards away from our apartment in the clinic. All I could think was, *God, where are You? ...I have nothing to ease his pain and suffering...* My visits were daily, sometimes two or three times a day. Mayra and Pepe's parents were like strangely "unreal people"...so glad to see me, smiling, but I could never figure out why...I came with nothing to offer but myself. One day toward the end, I entered the bedroom, and I was sure Pepe was now delirious, which struck me, paralyzed me...and Mayra caught my eye and pursed her lips, reminding me; I was embarrassed—I had failed to give Pepe the customary kiss on the cheek I always did...catching myself,

I quickly bent and gave Pepe not a customary kiss but of deep love not only for this precious couple but also for God permitting me to walk through this valley of inexpressible pain and poverty. As I write this, currents of tears and grieving come now after many years. I can attest to the Holy Spirit within keeping me focused outward as a compassionate nurse and friend...and now I am able to grieve, grieve deeply.

Pepe endured much longer than medically projected. The day he left his earthly shell, Mayra said they wanted Pepe embalmed. (This is not customary among the impoverished. They are buried the next day for obvious reasons.) Dr. Jorge Rodriguez said he was experienced and could embalm Pepe, and I was to assist. Unfortunately, Mayra had turned off Pepe's IV, which would have been used to inject the embalming fluid... Pepe's lifeless head drooped over my shoulder as gastric fluid flowed from his mouth...

The overnight watch at the home is traditional—a large canopy immediately outside of his parents' home was erected with chairs. Throughout the night, family and friends came to pay respects and share their love and grieving with the family...as Pepe's body lay in state. As also customary, the next day was the church service and then carrying the coffin to the cemetery... Not to the humble Florón Cemetery but to Pepe's aunt's cemetery in Portoviejo, which had a plot at the incredibly beautiful "La Paz Cemetery"; I have never seen a more beautiful cemetery. The walk of friends and family carrying the coffin (also customary) was five miles in unspeakable heat and humidity that Pepe's friends endured as they carried his coffin on their shoulders and somberly walked with Pepe one last time.

Mayra never dated until seven years later at the insistence of friends. Incredibly, this man had lost his wife from the same neuroendocrine tumor that took Pepe's life, currently leaving Jorge Salvatierra Alvarez with nine-year-old and three-year-old daughters. Their youngest child was in-utero at the time when his wife's rare tumor was discovered. We attended Mayra and Jorge's wedding, and two years later, Mayra became a mom besides being a stepmom. I continue to see her, Jorge, and their three children in church. The family looks incredibly happy... Thank You, my Lord Jesus.

This entire episode took a piece of my life that showed me an unwavering faithfulness of God amidst severe pain and incredible poverty. I continue to wonder if materialism does not often inhibit and/or block fortifying my own spiritual maturation.

"Yea, though I walk through the valley of the shadow of death, I will fear no evil; "For You are with me..."
(Psalm 23:4a, NKJV)

Mayra, Jorge and
their three daughters.

CHAPTER 18

Twenty Sewing Machines

Miraculously, I came into possession of twenty used sewing machines. Years ago, someone told me about a lady that collected used sewing machines; she did not do anything with them, just collected them. I contacted Michelle Zoetewey, and sure enough, Michelle had a huge plastic-covered Quonset Hut in her backyard that housed at least two hundred stacked-up sewing machines; she was willing to donate twenty. Lavonne Lintelmann at church told me about a man in north Denver that repaired sewing machines. So I piled all twenty sewing machines in the car and headed for this repair shop... By exchanging parts, he got sixteen wonderfully working machines out of the twenty, and all he asked was a tax write-off. Thus, sixteen mint working machines were on their way to Ecuador on our second shipment. (This was better than Christmas!)

Fast forward to 2018. For some reason, *Señora* Yolanda de Avila, executive president for the Dr. Oswaldo Loor Foundation (an exceptional, well-established eye clinic in Portoviejo), came to see and introduce me to a lady who was a social worker. (I never did quite figure out why.) Somehow, we got on the topic of sewing machines. Yolanda suggested we have a sewing class. "I would definitely need an instructor," I replied. She immediately tapped out numbers on her cell phone and called a professional seamstress she knew, and we connected. A month later, we had sixteen people signed up for a six-week beginners' sewing class; Pastor Gruezo graciously said I could use the school's desks (since the school was no longer open) to set the sewing machines.

María was a delightful teacher, to say the least. They use no pattern but measured, measured, measured to get the article of clothing to fit *perfectly* on the wearer. (No surprise, I took María home once, and of course, she insisted I meet her family, meaning her brother, mother, and her daughter. And I saw the perfectly handsome tuxedos and men's suits her brother made. Their business was a small room connected to their home like many small businesses are in Ecuador.) Our sewing class was held in the very large storage building behind the clinic. I loved going out to the class to see how it was going.

The ladies were bubbling with chatter! The *tela* (cloth) was donated previously from our church. So the ladies had a big choice in fabric to make their first skirt. We were able to hold the six-week class twice prior to the COVID crisis.

At the end of the class, the ladies surprised me and said they wanted a fashion show and luncheon. They would bring the food. Well, they did not exactly "walk the red carpet ramp"; they walked a cracked, uneven sidewalk, and they exploded with glamor and dignity! Hopefully, we can do this in the future... It was music to my ears to hear these ladies having so much laughter and fun that their arduous lives rarely offer!

> *"You will show me the path of life; In Your presence*
> *is fullness of joy; At Your right hand are pleasures*
> *forevermore."*
>
> (Psalm 16:11, NKJV)

CHAPTER 19

April 2016, Earthquake

On April 16, 2016, I was with our son and family in Portland, Oregon, when we heard of the earthquake in Ecuador that rocked and leveled the coastal town of Pedernales to the ground; the quake was 7.8 on the Richter scale with the epicenter seventeen miles offshore. The original earthquake was followed by severe aftershocks on May 19 and July 10. Portoviejo (a city with a population of 250,000, of which Florón is a suburb) was 120 miles south of Pedernales and lost over half of its major buildings in the central part of the city. Hearing of the original quake, I took the next flight home to Denver, and Richard was packed and ready for us to head for Houston, on to Quito, and then to Manta, where the entire airport, including the control tower, was gone.

Prior to our arrival, the community of Florón frantically stormed our mini water production plant. Gates around the compound were quickly closed, and authorities were called in to manage the desperate, out-of-control crowd. Dr. Silvia closed the clinic, and all personnel went to aid the water technicians and speed up water bottling production. Thankfully, police authorities took impressive action in crowd control.

Previously stated, Florón is a suburb of Portoviejo. Surprisingly, Florón had minimal damage except for the chapel in Florón 8, which lost walls. Portoviejo was painfully an entirely different story. The most devastated areas were blocked off and guarded for obvious reasons. However, being an American sometimes grants special "privileges." We were allowed in to survey the cement carnage of many, many blocks of central Portoviejo.

This was the first time I had actually "been there" to observe such massive damage. There are and, in the past, have been continual tremors in Ecuador; previously, Richard and I have been "shaken and awakened" by a 5.0 quake plus milder ones periodically. The morning of this particular quake, our neighbors in Florón had taken their toddler to the doctor in Portoviejo, and as usual, the government clinic did not have in stock the medicine prescribed. They continued to a pharmacy—a pharmacy destined for destruction, which claimed the lives of parents and child. Days after the initial quake, other major Portoviejo buildings continued to crumble. Buen Samaritano staff made and distributed care packages to Portoviejo residents.

"Hell and Destruction are never full...."
(Proverbs 27:20, NKJV)

CHAPTER 20

Indigenous Uprising

In October of 2019, a medical mission was organized by Just Jump's executive director, Cara Harrington. Cara had organized and blessed "Yo Te Amo" and Buen Samaritano Clinic with two previous missions that were beautifully executed at various underserved communities in the Manabí Province.

Precisely at the same time of the team's arrival at the new Quito Airport, the Ecuadorian Indigenous people initiated a transportation strike that paralyzed the country. In smaller cities, including Portoviejo/Florón, buses and taxis are the main means of transportation; neither moved. In the Portoviejo area, all arteries in and out of the city were blocked by taxis. Even worse, the exhausted US mission team could not transfer from the Quito Airport to their hotel. Thus, they slept in the airport.

By the grapevine, we heard taxi drivers were going home at 2 a.m. Thus, Richard and I zoomed out of Florón/Portoviejo to the Manta Airport and scoped out a hotel in case we were unable to transport the team from the Manta Airport to Florón, a forty-five-minute drive... The hotel was about a mile walk from the airport. (I just sank imagining this team toting all their luggage and supplies from the airport to the hotel.)

Divine intervention strikes again! Many were aware of our upcoming plight... We were contacted and assured by police that if there were problems transporting the team from the Manta Airport (because of unwilling taxi drivers refusing to move), we should contact the police. The team was honored and allowed to pass the next day; however, one of our sites scheduled to hold a clinic had to be canceled because the strike continued, and there was only one way to get to this church; thus, we held an extra day of clinic at Buen Samaritano. (I still wonder if any of that fortuitous group of individuals ever went on another mission trip.)

> *"I press toward the goal for the prize of the upward*
> *call of God in Jesus Christ."*
> (Philippians 3:14, NKJV)

CHAPTER 21

Building a House

Mission team individuals often develop relationships during their stay at Buen Samaritano Clinic and Water. Ecuadorians are friendly, warm-hearted people. And, of course, mission teams extend themselves, especially to the many curious children who are ever-present. On occasion, these friendships blossom beyond the one time in Florón, and people return to the joy of previous acquaintances.

This was true of a particular family...the one couple in a larger family had hoped and planned to bring one of the girls, Delores, to the USA to attend college. Sadly, all their efforts proved futile. However, the family at large was not deterred by that disappointment. Ultimately, the entire family of two generations packed their bags and headed for Ecuador. Their mission? To build a house for Delores, Ariana, and their parents, Pastor Meza and Bella.

Let me interject that the Meza family lived in, by American standards, *less* than a shack in Florón 8. During one of my visits, Delores and Ariana wanted me to see their bedroom that was not part of the "house." So I climbed a very rickety ladder up to their room, which had walls of bamboo slats that I could easily see through to the sky.

I could not imagine what it was like when monsoon rains came. They must have gotten drenched! I remember Delores telling me how in another building, which would be the "house" (kitchen with a dirt floor), she was cleaning, and she saw something move...investigation uncovered a snake. However, this one was not poisonous as the one Bella encountered in their outhouse...a four-foot-long "Equis." I had heard tales of the "Equis," and if bitten, you left this life within your next step.

Amazingly, this family always looked immaculate, and despite this less than humble home, a small chapel next to their home had been built for Pastor Meza and Belle to minister and evangelize to the people and children in this area. Florón 8 is known for severe poverty and dangerous corruption. Currently, many Venezuelans are moving into the area, which has caused tension...but some do attend the services at the chapel.

Excuse me, I digressed. Hopefully, you get the picture that the fact that the family from the USA returned to build a home for the Meza family was an incredible outpouring of indescribable proportions of love and compassion.

The home was not 100 percent finished by the time they left, but little remained...and now, as time marches on, the Meza family continues to teach and worship at the little chapel; Pastor Meza works as the day guard at the clinic; Delores finished at the university (thanks to the same family supporting her), and she continues to manage the clinic office...and at night they all return to sleep in a home that defies monsoon rains from entering.

CHAPTER 22

Invasion of the Venezuelans

As Venezuela went from the wealthiest nation in the world to being destroyed by multiple forms of government and political corruption and to the basic need of food for survival, Venezuelan people exited en mass. Ecuador was one of the main recipients of the three million people fighting for survival. In our area (Portoviejo being the major city), we found multiple individuals standing amidst traffic on every main thoroughfare. They wash your car windows for any amount...profusely thanking you for a quarter. Frequently, you will see the wife and children sitting on the curbside in heavily traveled streets where the husband found "income" was the most lucrative. Colombia and Peru have also experienced this same influx of migrants.

Dra. Lidia Moscoso is a pediatrician who shared major concerns, especially for health reasons. Often the poverty of Venezuelans meant crowding twenty to thirty people in a one-room apartment. Obviously, such circumstances were the breeding ground for hepatitis, malaria, typhoid, and a plethora of viruses, not of which the least was multiple strains of COVID.

The Venezuelan situation compounded our concerns as they began to infiltrate the Florón community of poverty. Thus, Buen Samaritano Clinic and Emanuel Church next door to the clinic joined forces to hold a clothes drive. Clothes were donated from the foundation's American support church... Massive contributions came to our church, Cherry Creek Presbyterian Church! Donations we carried in duffle bags and luggage down to Ecuador. We set up a weekend clinic, especially for the Venezuelans, for medical care, clothes, and, yes...a hot meal. I was timid in asking Pastor Gruezo and his wife, Jacqueline, if the church could make a meal if we provided whatever ingredients they wanted.

Really now...what I was asking was *impoverished* people to make a meal for *impoverished* immigrants. Would that be called an oxymoron? Well, it astounded me, whatever you call it...perhaps "heavenly sunshine." Pastor Gruezo and Jacqueline did not hesitate for a moment, "Sure! No problem. Let us go over now and talk to Sister María."

Hopefully, you have absorbed or recognized the amazing power of the Holy Spirit... If you are attuned or accustomed to listening to the loudness of the world, I doubt you can "catch" or experience this gentle, fragrant Counselor and Guide. Obviously, I required multiple situations along the way for His Spirit to direct my path...Obviously, I was often stubborn, unbelieving, or just perplexed on what to do.

However, I have always prayed that I never quenched the Holy Spirit. And whether you and I are willing to acknowledge it or not, it is the Holy Spirit that directs all that is good, that is beautiful, that is kind, that is righteous... I know this to be profoundly true.

Pulling together twenty-five years is impossible. I keep thinking, *Oh darn, I should include...* And the precious memories reel on and on. However, what an outlandish thought. From beginning to end, the Bible clearly describes the participation of the Holy Spirit from Genesis through Revelation. Meaning the continual presence of the Holy Spirit—recognized or unrecognized—exists in each of our lives that follow Jesus Christ:

> ..."He will give you another Helper, that He may abide with you forever—the Spirit of truth, whom the world cannot receive, because it neither sees Him nor knows Him; but you know Him, for He dwells with you and will be in you. I will not leave you orphans; I will come to you."
>
> John 14:16b–18 (NKJV)

My reflection of twenty-five years of working in Ecuador is not the *initiation* of the Holy Spirit in my life...I just did not recognize this spiritual force previously that was *always* there! I was not aware of this power within, and I wonder how many Christians walk as I did. Do you?

CHAPTER 23

Education

Please let me unload wonderful educational happenings over these twenty-five years... Now, this may not seem like a big deal or impressive to you, but I am telling you, *this is a big deal*...

» Early in Dra. Silvia's career at Buen Samaritano, she asked to take a two-year course in sexual health and reproduction, which benefited women of all ages.

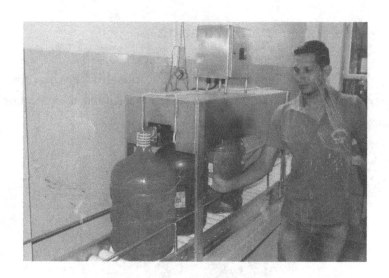

» Water tech José was hired with the agreement that he would attend night classes to complete his GED, which he did... Plus, we sent him to take a driver's ed course so he could get a driver's license and help with brief trips in the area. Later, he borrowed money from us so he could take a truck driver's class and get a commercial driver's license. (This did mean we lost an excellent *jefe* water technician—but hey, it was great! He told me his wife now wanted to go to college.)

» Come to think of it, going *waaaaay* back, Carlos was a bright young man working in the water. We also sent him to driver's ed. Richard did offer to send him to college, but he was focused on attending the police academy...and he did... The entrance requirements were not easy. The academy was rough, to say the least, and at one point, it was closed due to an infestation of sand flies that infected students' skin. Then, the government ran out of funding, and all the cadets had to provide for their own meals. So a Colorado family donated money for Carlos's food expenses.

» Our petite nurse assistant, Angelita, at sixty-five, asked if she could leave at noon on Fridays to take a class to get her GED. She and I practiced English, her toughest class. We laughed ourselves silly as I helped her practice English pronunciations that tied her tongue in knots. And at sixty-eight, Angelita graduated the "most senior" in her class and was admired by her family and her Buen Samaritano family.

» Diana (Dee-ana) has one year and eight months to finish nursing school, and it has been a struggle. And Botchi just graduated in business administration and has fulfilled her father's, Pastor Eduardo Gruezo, hopes. (Pastor Gruezo unexpectedly passed away early last year.) Both Diana and Botchi were gratefully supported by American donors.

» Our dentist, Dra. Karolina, flew to Brazil every six weeks for two years for an advanced course in all areas of dental restoration.

» Fabricio (our custodian) also took the class for a truck driver's license but then decided he would be away from his family too much. However, US Lawyer Candy McCune from our church came to teach mediation steps (from "Peacemakers") to our staff and noticed a "special something" about Fabricio and encouraged him to begin law school. She helped put him through five grueling years of law school while he kept his full-time job at the clinic. He completed law school in May 2021. Please stand up and cheer for this young man!

» Oops! Almost forgot "Loly" (Delores). She was funded at the private university by a compassionate couple, Dean and Jennifer Markham, that came on multiple missions to Ecuador and became well acquainted with Loly and her family. She also kept up her full-time job at the clinic and graduated in business administration this spring, 2021. (We are all thankful she remains "administrating" in our Buen Samaritano Clinic office.)

» Hopefully, I have not missed anyone; if this book is ever published, the staff will be excited to have their names in print as they should be for their godly character and accomplishments...with, I must add, compassionate American Christians guided by the Holy Spirit.

"Restore to me the joy of Your salvation And uphold me by Your generous Spirit."

(Psalm 51:12, NKJV)

ACKNOWLEDGMENTS

The support of family and friends, board members past and present, and especially Dottie McGuire and my mom, who prayed for me through the past twenty-five years. I lift each of you as God's gift to the people of El Florón and my increased awareness of the power of the Holy Spirit. All proceeds from this book go to Buen Samaritano Clinic and Water.

> *"I thank my God upon every remembrance of you,..."*
> (Philippians 1:3, NKJV)

For more information on this ministry or to contact go to www.fyta.org